Tulsi Gabbard: A Journey of Conviction and Courage

In the heart of the Pacific, under the gentle sway of Hawaiian breezes, Tulsi Gabbard began her journey, a tale woven with threads of resilience and conviction. Born on April 12, 1981, she emerged into a world ripe with promise and possibility.

From her earliest days, Tulsi exuded a spirit of determination. At the tender age of 21, she embarked on her political odyssey, winning a seat in the Hawaii House of Representatives, a feat that showcased her precocious intellect and unwavering dedication to public service.

Yet, Tulsi's commitment to duty extended beyond the hallowed halls of legislation. In 2004, she answered the call of duty, donning the uniform of the Hawaii Army National Guard. As the sands of Iraq whispered tales of turmoil, Tulsi stood as a beacon of hope, serving in a field medical unit with unwavering courage.
Her valor knew no bounds, as she later found herself stationed in Kuwait, leading as an Army Military Police platoon leader from 2008 to 2009. Through the trials of war, Tulsi emerged as a steadfast leader, her resolve unshaken by the crucible of conflict.

In 2013, Tulsi's journey took a historic turn as she became the first Hindu member of the United States Congress, representing Hawaii's 2nd congressional district. This milestone marked not only a personal triumph but also a testament to the rich tapestry of diversity that defines America.
Throughout her tenure in Congress, Tulsi remained an unwavering voice for change, fearlessly advocating for her convictions. From her perch as vice chair of the Democratic National Committee, she championed causes close to her heart, earning admiration for her principled stance.
Yet, Tulsi's path was not without its controversies. Her outspoken criticism of the Obama administration's handling of radical Islam sparked heated debate, as she stood firm in her beliefs, unswayed by political pressure.

In 2020, Tulsi embarked on a new chapter, throwing her hat into the ring for the Democratic nomination in the presidential election. Her campaign, fueled by a fervent opposition to military interventionism, captured the imagination of many, even

As the sun sets on the horizon of political discourse, Tulsi Gabbard's story continues to unfold, each chapter imbued with the echoes of her unwavering convictions.

In the aftermath of her departure from the Democratic Party, Tulsi embarked on a new chapter of her political journey, navigating uncharted waters with the poise and determination that have come to define her. Embracing her role as an independent voice, she embarked on a mission to bridge the gaping divides that threaten to tear the fabric of American society asunder.

With each passing day, Tulsi found herself drawn further into the fray, her voice resonating across the political spectrum. From the hallowed halls of Congress to the bustling streets of Main Street, USA, she tirelessly championed causes close to her heart, refusing to be confined by the shackles of partisan politics.

In the midst of a world gripped by uncertainty and turmoil, Tulsi emerged as a steadfast advocate for unity and understanding. Through her words and deeds, she sought to transcend the petty squabbles that too often define contemporary politics, forging bonds of solidarity that stretched across ideological divides.

As the 2024 presidential election loomed on the horizon, whispers of speculation swirled around Tulsi's name, with many wondering whether she would once again throw her hat into the ring. Yet, amidst the clamor of political pundits and prognosticators, Tulsi remained characteristically coy, her intentions known only to herself.

Regardless of what the future may hold, one thing remains certain: Tulsi Gabbard's journey is far from over. As she continues to navigate the turbulent waters of American politics, her unwavering commitment to principle and her unyielding spirit of conviction will serve as guiding beacons, illuminating the path forward in an uncertain world.

Tulsi Gabbard: A Tapestry of Heritage and Identity

In the verdant embrace of the Pacific, amidst the whispers of tropical breezes, Tulsi Gabbard entered the world on April 12, 1981, in Leloaloa, Ma'opūtasi County, on the enchanting island of Tutuila, American Samoa. She arrived as the fourth child of Carol and Mike Gabbard, nestled within a vibrant tapestry of Samoan and European ancestry.

In the kaleidoscope of her upbringing, Tulsi's life was infused with the richness of multiculturalism. Her mother, a devout Hindu, bestowed upon her children names steeped in the sacred traditions of India. Tulsi, derived from Sanskrit, symbolized holy basil, revered as an earthly embodiment of the divine. Under the gentle guidance of her parents, Tulsi was immersed in the teachings of the Vaishnava Hindu tradition, finding solace and spiritual nourishment within its embrace.

As the gentle currents of destiny carried her family across the vast expanse of the Pacific, Tulsi's journey led her to the shores of Hawaii, where she would come of age amidst the splendor of its azure seas and verdant landscapes. Here, she found herself enveloped in the warm embrace of island life, her soul intertwined with the rhythm of the waves and the whisper of the trade winds.

From an early age, Tulsi's spirit burned bright with a passion for service and advocacy. Inspired by the teachings of her faith and the example set by her parents, she embarked on a journey of self-discovery and enlightenment. Guided by the principles of compassion and integrity, she sought to make a difference in the world around her.

In the hallowed halls of education, Tulsi's intellect shone brightly, illuminating the path to a future filled with promise and possibility. Though her early years were marked by the challenges of homeschooling and a brief stint at an all-girls boarding school in the Philippines, she emerged with a thirst for knowledge and a hunger for success.

Fuelled by her passion for martial arts and a desire to make a difference in her community, Tulsi forged ahead, carving out a path that would lead her to the pinnacle of political power. In 2002, at the age of 21, she made history as the youngest person ever elected to the Hawaii House of Representatives, a testament to her tenacity and resolve.

As she ascended the ranks of political prominence, Tulsi's journey was marked by both triumph and controversy. Her work with organizations founded by her father, including Stand Up For America and The Alliance for Traditional Marriage and Values, thrust her into the spotlight, sparking heated debate and passionate discourse.

Yet, through it all, Tulsi remained steadfast in her commitment to serving others and fighting for the causes she held dear. In 2009, she graduated from Hawaii Pacific University with a Bachelor of Science in Business Administration, a testament to her unwavering dedication to excellence and achievement.

As Tulsi's journey continues to unfold, one thing remains certain: her story is a testament to the power of heritage, identity, and the unwavering spirit of determination. In a world fraught with uncertainty and division, she stands as a beacon of hope and inspiration, a testament to the enduring power of the human spirit to overcome adversity and forge a brighter tomorrow.

In April 2003, amidst the bustling corridors of the Hawaii State Legislature, Tulsi Gabbard made a decision that would forever alter the course of her life. With unwavering resolve and a deep-seated sense of duty, she enlisted in the Hawaii Army National Guard, embarking on a journey that would test her mettle and forge her character in the crucible of conflict.

In July 2004, Tulsi's path led her to the sun-scorched sands of Iraq, where she served with distinction as a specialist with the Medical Company, 29th Support Battalion, 29th Infantry Brigade Combat Team. Amidst the chaos of war, she tended to the wounded and comforted the afflicted, her courage and compassion shining brightly amidst the darkness of battle.

Throughout her 12-month tour, Tulsi distinguished herself as a beacon of hope amidst the turmoil of war-torn Iraq. Stationed at Logistical Support Area Anaconda, she faced the harsh realities of combat with unyielding resolve, her commitment to her comrades and her country unwavering in the face of adversity.

Upon her return from Iraq in 2005, Tulsi faced a difficult decision. Despite her burgeoning political career, she chose to prioritize her military service, forgoing reelection to the state legislature to continue her service in the Hawaii Army National Guard.

In March 2007, Tulsi's dedication to duty led her to the hallowed halls of the Alabama Military Academy, where she graduated from the Accelerated Officer Candidate School. Commissioned as a second lieutenant, she was assigned to the 29th Brigade Special Troops Battalion, 29th Infantry Brigade Combat Team, this time serving as an Army Military Police officer.

From 2008 to 2009, Tulsi found herself stationed in the deserts of Kuwait, where she once again distinguished herself as a trailblazer and a leader. As one of the first women to enter a Kuwaiti military facility, she shattered barriers and defied expectations, earning the respect and admiration of her peers and superiors alike.

Throughout her military career, Tulsi's bravery and dedication were recognized with numerous accolades, including the Combat Medical Badge and the Meritorious Service Medal. On October 12, 2015, she stood tall and proud as she was promoted from the rank of captain to major, a testament to her unwavering commitment to excellence and leadership.

Yet, even as Tulsi's star rose in the political arena, her dedication to her military service never wavered. In June 2020, she transferred to the 351st Civil Affairs Command, a California-based United States Army Reserve unit, continuing her service to her country with distinction and honor.

However, Tulsi's military service was not without its challenges. In August 2018, she found herself embroiled in controversy when the Hawaii Army National Guard instructed her to remove a video of herself in uniform from her campaign's Facebook page, citing violations of military ethics rules. Undeterred, Tulsi pledged to work closely with the Department of Defense to ensure compliance with all regulations.

In October 2020, Tulsi made the difficult decision to leave the Hawaii Army National Guard and join the Army Reserve with a California-based unit, continuing her journey of service and sacrifice with a new sense of purpose and determination.

On July 4, 2021, Tulsi's dedication and commitment were once again recognized as she was promoted to the rank of lieutenant colonel, a testament to her unwavering devotion to her country and her fellow soldiers.

As Tulsi's journey as a soldier continues to unfold, one thing remains certain: her unwavering courage, integrity, and commitment to duty serve as a shining example to us all, reminding us of the true meaning of service and sacrifice.

In 2002, amidst the verdant landscapes and gentle trade winds of Hawaii, Tulsi Gabbard embarked on a journey that would make history. Following a redistricting that reshaped the political landscape, she emerged as a beacon of hope and change, capturing the imagination of voters across the 42nd district of the Hawaii House of Representatives.

In a crowded Democratic primary, Tulsi's message of unity and progress resonated deeply with voters, propelling her to victory with a commanding plurality of 43% of the vote. Undeterred by the challenges that lay ahead, she forged ahead with unwavering determination, her sights set firmly on the path to victory.

In the general election that followed, Tulsi's momentum only continued to grow, as she secured an impressive 60.7% of the vote, defeating her Republican opponent, Alfonso Jimenez, with ease. At the tender age of 21, Tulsi shattered records and made history, becoming not only the youngest legislator ever elected in Hawaii's history but also the youngest woman ever elected to a U.S. state legislature.

As a member of the Hawaii House of Representatives, Tulsi wasted no time in making her mark on the political landscape. With a fierce commitment to her principles and an unwavering dedication to her constituents, she fearlessly led opposition to a state bill that would have legalized same-sex civil unions. Through her impassioned advocacy and steadfast leadership, she rallied Hawaiians to support the Federal Marriage Amendment, ensuring that state law would not be overridden by federal mandates on same-sex marriage.

Yet, even as Tulsi's star rose in the political firmament, her commitment to duty and service remained unwavering. In 2004, faced with the prospect of deployment to Iraq with the Army National Guard, Tulsi made the difficult decision to forgo reelection, putting the needs of her country above her own political aspirations.

Her opponent, Rida Cabanilla, called on Tulsi to resign, citing concerns about her ability to effectively represent her district from overseas. Despite these challenges, Tulsi remained resolute, announcing her decision not to campaign for a second term and allowing the democratic process to unfold.

In a testament to her character and dedication, Tulsi's name remained on the ballot, a symbol of her unwavering commitment to her constituents and her country. Though she may have stepped away from the political arena for a time, her legacy endured, a testament to the indelible mark she had left on the Hawaii House of Representatives and the hearts of those she served.

After her return from her second deployment to the Middle East in 2009, Tulsi Gabbard embarked on a new chapter of her journey, setting her sights on the Honolulu City Council. With the retirement of City Councilman Rod Tam, the seat for the 6th district lay vacant, beckoning for a leader to step forward and champion the needs of the community.

In the crowded field of the 10-candidate nonpartisan open primary in September 2010, Tulsi's message of progress and innovation struck a chord with voters, propelling her to a decisive victory with 26.8% of the vote. Undeterred by the challenges that lay ahead, she forged ahead with unwavering determination, her sights set firmly on the path to victory.

In the runoff election that followed on November 2, Tulsi faced off against Sesnita Moepono, her opponent in a contest that would determine the future direction of Honolulu's City Council. With the spirit of aloha as her guiding light, Tulsi emerged triumphant once again, securing victory with 49.5% of the vote.

As a member of the Honolulu City Council, Tulsi wasted no time in making her presence felt, introducing measures aimed at fostering positive change and improving the lives of her constituents. Recognizing the importance of supporting small businesses, she introduced a measure to help food truck vendors by loosening parking restrictions, ensuring that entrepreneurs had the opportunity to thrive and succeed in the vibrant tapestry of Honolulu's culinary landscape.

Yet, Tulsi's tenure on the City Council was not without its controversies. Her introduction of Bill 54, a measure that authorized city workers to confiscate personal belongings stored on public property with 24 hours notice to its owner, sparked heated debate and passionate opposition from groups such as the American Civil Liberties Union (ACLU) and Occupy Hawai'i. Despite these challenges, Tulsi remained steadfast in her commitment to addressing the needs of the community and finding innovative solutions to complex issues.

In the face of adversity, Tulsi's determination and resilience shone brightly, as Bill 54 ultimately passed and became City Ordinance 1129, a testament to her unwavering commitment to serving the people of Honolulu and her steadfast belief in the power of positive change.

Though her time on the Honolulu City Council was relatively brief, Tulsi's impact was profound, leaving an indelible mark on the landscape of local politics and the hearts of those she served. As she set her sights on new horizons and continued her journey of service and leadership, one thing remained certain: Tulsi Gabbard would always be a voice for change, a beacon of hope in a world in need of compassion and courage.

In the corridors of power, amidst the hustle and bustle of political maneuvering, Tulsi Gabbard's journey took an electrifying turn in early 2011. With the announcement by Mazie Hirono, the incumbent Democratic U.S. Representative for Hawaii's 2nd congressional district, that she would run for the United States Senate, a vacuum emerged, beckoning for a new leader to step forward and champion the needs of the people.

In May 2011, Tulsi Gabbard answered the call, announcing her candidacy for Hirono's House seat. Despite facing stiff competition, including the well-known Democratic Mayor of Honolulu, Mufi Hannemann, Tulsi's message of hope and change resonated deeply with voters. In a stunning upset, she emerged victorious in the six-way primary, securing a decisive win with 55% of the vote. The Honolulu Star-Advertiser hailed her triumph as an "improbable rise from a distant underdog to victory," a testament to her resilience and determination.

With the primary behind her, Tulsi set her sights on the general election, where she faced off against Republican Kawika Crowley. In a resounding victory that sent shockwaves through the political establishment, Tulsi emerged triumphant, capturing a staggering 80.6% of the vote and making history as the first voting Samoan-American and the first Hindu member of Congress.

As she took her place among the esteemed ranks of the 113th Congress, Tulsi wasted no time in making her presence felt. In December 2012, she applied to be considered for appointment to the U.S. Senate seat vacated by the death of Daniel Inouye, earning praise from prominent mainland Democrats for her leadership and vision. Though she was not ultimately selected by the Democratic Party of Hawaii, her ambition and determination were undimmed.

In March 2013, Tulsi embarked on a mission to enact meaningful change, introducing the Helping Heroes Fly Act, a measure aimed at improving airport security screenings for severely wounded veterans. Her tireless advocacy bore fruit, as the bill passed Congress and was signed into law by President Barack Obama, a testament to Tulsi's commitment to those who have served their country with honor and distinction.

Additionally, Tulsi introduced the House version of the Military Justice Improvement Act, further cementing her reputation as a champion for the brave men and women of the United States Armed Forces. With each passing day, Tulsi's star continued to rise, her unwavering dedication to her constituents and her country earning her accolades and admiration from across the political spectrum.

As she embarked on her first term in Congress, Tulsi Gabbard stood poised on the brink of greatness, her journey as a public servant just beginning, yet already marked by triumph and promise. With the future stretching out before her like an open road, one thing remained certain: Tulsi Gabbard was destined for greatness, a rising star in the hallowed halls of Congress.

As the dawn broke on a new era in American politics, Tulsi Gabbard embarked on her second term in the hallowed halls of Congress with a sense of purpose and determination that burned brighter than ever before. With the resounding mandate of her constituents behind her, she stood ready to build upon the foundation of progress she had laid during her first term, championing the needs of the people with unwavering dedication and resolve.

In the 2014 United States House of Representatives elections in Hawaii's 2nd district, Tulsi once again faced off against her opponent, Kawika Crowley, in a contest that would once again test the strength of her support among the voters. In a landslide victory that underscored her popularity and effectiveness as a representative, Tulsi emerged triumphant, securing an impressive 78.7% of the vote and reaffirming her commitment to serving the people of Hawaii.

Yet, Tulsi's impact extended far beyond the borders of her home state. Teaming up with Senator Mazie Hirono, she introduced a bill to award the Congressional Gold Medal to Filipinos and Filipino American veterans who had fought valiantly in World War II. Their tireless advocacy bore fruit, as the bill passed Congress with overwhelming bipartisan support and was signed into law by President Obama in December 2016, honoring the brave men and women who had sacrificed so much in service to their country.

Additionally, Tulsi introduced Talia's Law, a groundbreaking measure aimed at preventing child abuse and neglect on military bases. Recognizing the importance of protecting the most vulnerable members of our society, she worked tirelessly to garner support for the bill, marshaling her colleagues in Congress to join her in the fight for justice and accountability. Her efforts were rewarded when Talia's Law passed Congress and was signed into law by President Obama in December 2016, ensuring that military families would have the resources and support they needed to keep their children safe.

As she continued her journey of service and advocacy, Tulsi Gabbard stood as a shining example of leadership and integrity in Congress, her unwavering commitment to the people she served earning her admiration and respect from across the political spectrum. With each passing day, she reaffirmed her dedication to the timeless values of justice, equality, and compassion, leaving an indelible mark on the fabric of American politics and inspiring countless others to follow in her footsteps.

As she looked to the future with hope and optimism, one thing remained certain: Tulsi Gabbard's journey was far from over, and her legacy as a tireless champion for the people would endure for generations to come.

As the nation stood at the precipice of a new chapter in its history, Tulsi Gabbard entered her third term in the United States House of Representatives with a renewed sense of purpose and determination. With the resounding support of her constituents behind her, she embarked on a journey to continue the fight for justice, equality, and progress in the hallowed halls of Congress.

In the 2016 United States House of Representatives elections in Hawaii's 2nd district, Tulsi once again emerged victorious, securing an overwhelming mandate from the people she served. Facing off against Republican nominee Angela Kaaihue, she captured an impressive 81.2% of the vote, reaffirming her status as a beloved and effective representative of the people.

With her reelection secured, Tulsi wasted no time in getting to work on behalf of her constituents and the American people. In 2017, she introduced the Off Fossil Fuels (OFF) Act, a groundbreaking piece of legislation aimed at transitioning away from fossil fuel sources of energy to 100% clean energy by 2035. With a vision for a sustainable and environmentally-conscious future, Tulsi sought to lead the way in combating climate change and preserving the planet for future generations.

In 2018, Tulsi continued her efforts to safeguard the integrity of America's democracy with the introduction of the Securing America's Election Act. Recognizing the importance of ensuring the fairness and transparency of our electoral process, she championed the use of paper ballots in all districts, a measure that would provide an auditable paper trail in the event of a recount. Her commitment to strengthening our democracy earned praise from Common Cause, a nonpartisan watchdog group, which endorsed the bill as a crucial step toward protecting the sanctity of the ballot box.

As she continued to advocate for the issues that mattered most to the people she served, Tulsi Gabbard stood as a beacon of progress and hope in the tumultuous landscape of American politics. With each passing day, she reaffirmed her commitment to building a brighter future for all Americans, inspiring countless others to join her in the fight for a more just, equitable, and sustainable world.

As the sun rose on a new day in American politics, Tulsi Gabbard embarked on her fourth term in the United States House of Representatives with a steadfast commitment to the principles of accountability, integrity, and service. With the resounding support of her constituents behind her, she stood ready to continue the fight for justice and progress in the hallowed halls of Congress.

In the 2018 United States House of Representatives elections in Hawaii's 2nd district, Tulsi once again secured victory, defeating Republican nominee Brian Evans with a commanding 77.4% of the vote. With her reelection secured, she reaffirmed her dedication to representing the interests of the people she served and fighting for the values she held dear.

Throughout her fourth term in Congress, Tulsi remained at the forefront of efforts to hold the executive branch accountable and reclaim Congress's constitutional authority to declare war. In September 2018, she joined forces with Representative Walter Jones to co-sponsor the No More Presidential Wars Act, a bold initiative aimed at ending presidential wars fought without congressional authorization. With a firm belief in the importance of congressional oversight and the rule of law, Tulsi sought to ensure that decisions regarding war and peace were made with the full participation of the legislative branch, as mandated by the Constitution.

Yet, even as she fought tirelessly for accountability and principle on the national stage, Tulsi faced challenges closer to home. In October 2019, she made the difficult decision not to seek reelection to the House in 2020, citing her presidential campaign and a desire to focus her energies on new endeavors. Her decision sparked criticism from opponents, including Hawaii State Senator Kai Kahele and former Hawaii governor Neil Abercrombie, who questioned her commitment to her constituents. However, Tulsi remained steadfast in her conviction that her presidential campaign offered a unique opportunity to elevate important issues and bring about meaningful change on a national scale.

In October 2020, Tulsi once again demonstrated her unwavering commitment to justice and principle with the introduction of a bill calling for the United States to drop criminal charges against Edward Snowden. Partnering with Congressman Matt Gaetz, she sought to ensure that Snowden, a whistleblower who had exposed government surveillance programs, would be treated fairly and justly under the law. Additionally, Tulsi introduced a similar bill, alongside Congressman Thomas Massie, aimed at securing the release of Julian Assange from prison in the United Kingdom, where he faced extradition to the United States. In championing these causes, Tulsi reaffirmed her belief in the importance of transparency, accountability, and respect for civil liberties in a democratic society.

As her fourth term in Congress drew to a close, Tulsi Gabbard's legacy as a principled leader and tireless advocate for justice and progress was secure. Though her time in the House was coming to an end, her journey of service and leadership was far from over, and her impact on the political landscape would endure for generations to come.

Committee Assignments

Committee on Homeland Security (2013–2014): Focusing on border and maritime security, this assignment underscored Gabbard's early commitment to addressing national security challenges, particularly those related to the United States' borders and points of entry.

Committee on Armed Services (2013–2021): With subcommittees on readiness and emerging threats and capabilities, her long-standing role here highlights her deep involvement in defense and military issues, reflecting her military background and interest in strengthening the armed forces and national defense.

Committee on Foreign Affairs (2013–2019): Through her work on the subcommittees for Asia and the Pacific and the Middle East and North Africa, Gabbard engaged in key geopolitical areas of interest, showcasing her focus on international diplomacy, regional stability, and U.S. foreign policy.

Committee on Financial Services (2019–2021): Her involvement in the subcommittees on national security, international development and monetary policy, and diversity and inclusion illustrates her interest in the intersection of financial policies with national security and her advocacy for inclusive economic growth and development.

Caucus Membership

Congressional Progressive Caucus: Membership here indicates Gabbard's alignment with progressive policy goals and initiatives, emphasizing her support for wide-ranging reforms across social, economic, and environmental domains.

Congressional Asian Pacific American Caucus: Reflecting her commitment to representing Asian Pacific American communities, this caucus membership aligns with her focus on diversity and inclusion in policy-making.

Congressional NextGen 9-1-1 Caucus: This indicates her interest in advancing emergency response technologies and improving public safety infrastructure to meet future challenges.

Medicare for All Caucus: Joining this caucus underscores her support for comprehensive healthcare reform, aiming to expand access to healthcare services for all Americans.

U.S.-Japan Caucus: Membership here highlights her interest in fostering strong bilateral relations between the United States and Japan, indicating a focus on diplomatic and strategic partnerships in Asia.

Tulsi Gabbard's tenure as a vice chair of the Democratic National Committee (DNC) was marked by both acclaim and controversy, as she navigated the intricacies of party politics and spoke out on issues of principle and process within the organization.

Elected unanimously to a four-year term on January 22, 2013, Gabbard assumed a prominent role within the DNC, representing the party at a national level and participating in key decision-making processes. However, her tenure took a contentious turn in September 2015 when she publicly criticized DNC chairwoman Debbie Wasserman Schultz's handling of the Democratic primary debates. Gabbard voiced concerns about the limited number of debates scheduled and the exclusionary criteria imposed on candidates, signaling a departure from party orthodoxy and advocating for a more inclusive and robust debate process.

These criticisms led to a strained relationship with party leadership, culminating in Gabbard's reported disinvitation from a Democratic debate in Las Vegas in October 2015. Feeling stifled and marginalized within the organization, she expressed frustration with what she perceived as an atmosphere of censorship and lack of transparency.

In a bold move, Gabbard resigned from her position as DNC vice chair on February 28, 2016, citing her desire to endorse Senator Bernie Sanders for the Democratic presidential nomination. Her decision to break ranks with party leadership and publicly endorse Sanders marked a significant moment in the 2016 election cycle, cementing her reputation as a principled and independent-minded politician willing to challenge the status quo.

Throughout the 2016 presidential campaign, Gabbard continued to advocate for reforms within the Democratic Party, launching a petition to end the use of superdelegates in the nomination process and endorsing Keith Ellison for DNC chair in subsequent elections.

Gabbard's tenure at the DNC, though relatively brief, left an indelible mark on the party's internal dynamics and underscored her commitment to principles of fairness, transparency, and democratic accountability. Despite facing pushback and criticism from within the party establishment, she remained steadfast in her convictions, paving the way for a more open and inclusive Democratic Party in the years to come.

Tulsi Gabbard's 2020 presidential campaign was a bold and unconventional journey that captured the attention of the nation, challenging the status quo and advocating for a platform grounded in anti-interventionist foreign policy and populist economic principles.

Officially launching her campaign in February 2019, Gabbard made history as the first female combat veteran to run for president. Her candidacy garnered significant interest and curiosity, with her foreign policy stance being described as anti-interventionist and her economic platform as populist by CNN.

Throughout the primary season, Gabbard faced both triumphs and challenges. Despite not meeting the polling threshold for the third presidential debate, she remained vocal in her criticism of the Democratic National Committee's qualification criteria, highlighting what she perceived as a lack of transparency in the process. Gabbard's participation in the fourth debate in October 2019 was marked by her accusations of media and party "rigging" of the election, though she ultimately chose to participate.

Gabbard's campaign stood out for its willingness to engage with diverse communities and confront contentious issues head-on. In July 2019, she became the sole presidential candidate to visit Puerto Rico and join protests calling for Governor Ricardo Rosselló's resignation, showcasing her commitment to grassroots activism and solidarity with marginalized communities.

However, her campaign was not without controversy. In October 2019, false reports emerged linking Gabbard to Russian interference efforts, leading to a public spat with former Secretary of State Hillary Clinton. Gabbard vehemently denied these allegations and filed a defamation lawsuit against Clinton, which she later dropped.

Despite the challenges, Gabbard's campaign achieved a historic milestone on March 3, 2020, when she earned two delegates in American Samoa, becoming the second woman of color and the first Asian-American and Pacific Islander presidential candidate to earn primary delegates in the Democratic Party's history.

On March 19, 2020, Gabbard made the decision to suspend her campaign and endorse former Vice President Joe Biden, signaling the end of her bid for the presidency. While her campaign ultimately fell short of securing the nomination, Gabbard's candidacy left an indelible mark on the political landscape, challenging conventional wisdom and advocating for a more inclusive and principled approach to governance.

After suspending her 2020 presidential campaign, Tulsi Gabbard remained active in various public and philanthropic endeavors, leveraging her platform to advocate for causes close to her heart and support candidates aligned with her values.

In May 2020, Gabbard endorsed Democratic candidate Isaac Wilson in his bid for election to the 63rd district of the South Carolina House of Representatives. Although Wilson ultimately did not win, Gabbard's endorsement highlighted her ongoing commitment to supporting candidates she believed in.

In June 2020, Gabbard demonstrated her philanthropic spirit by donating approximately $4,400 to Direct Relief and the Semper Fi & America's Fund. These funds were raised through the proceeds of excess merchandise sales from her campaign, showcasing her dedication to supporting charitable causes even after the conclusion of her presidential bid.

July 2020 saw Gabbard standing in solidarity with the family of Vanessa Guillén, a U.S. Army soldier who tragically fell victim to military sexual harassment and was later found murdered. Gabbard met with Guillén's family and attorney, Natalie Khawam, expressing her support for them and speaking out against sexual harassment and assault in the military.

In August 2020, Gabbard participated as a panelist in discussions on "Electability" during The 19th Represents Virtual Summit. She also held a press conference alongside Dr. Scott Miscovich, advocating for increased accountability within the Hawaii Department of Health regarding its handling of the COVID-19 crisis.

Throughout the year, Gabbard continued to engage with pressing social and political issues, including expressing concerns about the Netflix film "Cuties" and its potential implications for child exploitation.

In December 2020, Gabbard endorsed Nina Turner and donated funds through her Tulsi Aloha PAC to support Turner's campaign for the 2021 special election for Ohio's 11th congressional district, further underscoring her commitment to advancing progressive causes and supporting like-minded candidates.

Gabbard's post-presidential primary activities reflect her ongoing dedication to public service, advocacy for social justice, and support for candidates who share her vision for a better future.

After her congressional tenure, Tulsi Gabbard embarked on a dynamic post-congressional career, engaging in various media platforms and expressing her perspectives on critical political issues.

In January 2021, Gabbard ventured into the realm of podcasting with the launch of "This is Tulsi Gabbard," providing a platform to discuss a wide range of topics and share her insights with a broad audience.

Throughout the year, Gabbard made multiple appearances on Fox News programs, where she didn't shy away from expressing her opinions on prominent political figures and events. Notably, she criticized House Speaker Nancy Pelosi and labeled U.S. Representative Adam Schiff as a "domestic terrorist" for what she saw as his actions undermining constitutional rights in the aftermath of the storming of the U.S. Capitol in 2021.

In November 2021, Gabbard weighed in on the Virginia gubernatorial election, characterizing Republican Glenn Youngkin's victory over Democrat Terry McAuliffe as a win for all Americans, signaling her continued engagement in national political discourse.

In April 2022, Gabbard expressed her support for Florida's contentious Parental Rights Bill during an appearance on Hannity, indicating her alignment with certain conservative policy positions and her willingness to engage in public debates on divisive issues.

Continuing her involvement in conservative circles, Gabbard spoke at the Conservative Political Action Conference (CPAC) in 2022, drawing criticism from Hawaii Democrats for her alignment with conservative platforms.

In August 2022, Gabbard stepped into the role of fill-in host for "Tucker Carlson Tonight," further solidifying her presence in the media landscape and her willingness to engage in dialogue across various political spectrums.

Tulsi Gabbard's departure from the Democratic Party marked a significant shift in her political trajectory. On October 11, 2022, she took to Twitter to announce her decision, citing her disillusionment with the party's direction. Gabbard criticized what she termed as the party's "cowardly wokeness," accusations of "anti-white racism," hostility towards people of faith, and concerns about policies potentially leading to nuclear conflict.

In a swift move following her departure, Gabbard actively endorsed and campaigned for several Republican candidates in the 2022 midterm elections, signaling her alignment with a different political ideology.

Shortly thereafter, Gabbard entered into a professional relationship with Fox News, signing on as a paid contributor. Her presence on the network expanded rapidly, with appearances on various shows such as The Five, Outnumbered, Hannity, Jesse Watters Primetime, and Gutfeld!. She even served as a guest host on Tucker Carlson Tonight before the show's cancellation in 2023.

As political dynamics continued to evolve, speculation arose about Gabbard's future role in the Republican Party. With Donald Trump's re-entry into the 2024 Republican presidential primary, commentators speculated on the possibility of Gabbard being considered as a potential vice-presidential running mate. Some, including Greg Gutfeld of Gutfeld! on Fox News, even went as far as predicting her selection by Trump for the position.

Tulsi Gabbard's political positions reflect a mix of progressive and conservative views on various issues:

Drug Policy and Criminal Justice Reform:

Gabbard advocates for ending the war on drugs, legalizing marijuana, ending cash bail, and banning private prisons. She has introduced legislation like the Ending Federal Marijuana Prohibition Act and the Marijuana Opportunity Reinvestment and Expungement (MORE) Act.

Immigration:

She supports increased border security, halting certain visa programs, but also advocates for an easier path to citizenship for illegal immigrants and increasing skilled immigration.

Environment:

Gabbard protested against the construction of the Dakota Access Pipeline and introduced legislation to address environmental issues, such as the Off Fossil Fuels for a Better Future Act.

Foreign Affairs:

She has been critical of U.S. intervention in foreign wars, advocating for a non-interventionist approach. Gabbard's fact-finding mission to Syria and Lebanon garnered attention, and she has expressed skepticism about U.S. involvement in conflicts like those in Syria and Ukraine.

Healthcare and GMO Labeling:

Gabbard supports a national healthcare insurance program and has pushed for Medicaid eligibility for certain populations. She advocates for clear GMO labeling and has introduced legislation in this regard.

LGBT Issues:

While Gabbard has evolved on LGBT issues, apologizing for her past advocacy against same-sex marriage, she has faced criticism for her earlier views. She co-sponsored legislation to repeal the Defense of Marriage Act and received ratings from pro-LGBT organizations for her congressional terms.

First Impeachment of Donald Trump:

Gabbard voted "present" during the first impeachment of Donald Trump, citing concerns about the political nature of the proceedings and advocating for censure instead.

Parental Rights and Education:

Gabbard has endorsed legislation like the Protect Women's Sports Act, which seeks to define Title IX protections based on biological sex, and Florida's Parental Rights Bill, which forbids discussing sexual orientation and gender identity in certain school classrooms.

These positions demonstrate Gabbard's nuanced approach to various issues, combining elements of progressivism with more conservative stances on select topics.

Tulsi Gabbard's personal life reflects her commitment to her faith, health, and relationships:

Dietary Choices:

Gabbard is vegan, aligning with her values of compassion and sustainability.
Religious Beliefs:

As a Hindu, she follows the Gaudiya Vaishnavism tradition and considers herself a karma yogi, emphasizing selfless action and service.
Spiritual Practices:

Gabbard finds guidance in the Bhagavad Gita, a revered Hindu scripture, and took her oath of office using her personal copy of the text.
Marriage and Family:

She was previously married to Eduardo Tamayo, with whom she divorced in 2006. They cited the strains of military life as a contributing factor.
In 2015, Gabbard married Abraham Williams in a traditional Vedic wedding ceremony, reflecting her cultural heritage and spiritual beliefs.

Tulsi Gabbard has been recognized with several awards and honors for her contributions and dedication:

John F. Kennedy New Frontier Award: Presented on November 25, 2013, at Harvard's John F. Kennedy School of Government, in recognition of her advocacy for veterans' issues.

Elle Magazine's Women in Washington Power List: Honored by Elle magazine at the Italian Embassy in the United States on March 20, 2014, alongside other influential women in Washington.

National Association of Counties County Alumni Award: Received on February 26, 2015, for her unwavering commitment to the nation's counties.

Friend of the National Parks Award: Conferred on July 15, 2015, by the National Parks Conservation Association, acknowledging her support for preserving and protecting national parks.

Ho'ola Na Pua Advocacy Award: Presented on September 30, 2018, for her dedicated service and empowerment of human trafficking survivors in Hawaii.

Paul T. C. Loo Distinguished Alumni Award: Honored by Hawai'i Pacific University on October 16, 2018, recognizing her achievements as an alumna.

Tulsi Gabbard has authored several published works, including:

"Is Today the Day? (Edition-II)" (2021) - Published by Grand Central Publishing. ISBN: 9781455542321.

"Is Today the Day?" (2019) - Published by Grand Central Publishing. ISBN: 9781455542314.

"I am Tulsi Gabbard" (2019) - Published by Flippin Sweet Books

Made in United States
Troutdale, OR
05/03/2024